★SKILLS BUILDERS

Writing

LEVELS 3–5

Marie Lallaway, Tom Johns and Mig Bennett

RISING★STARS

PLEASE NOTE: THIS BOOK MAY NOT BE PHOTOCOPIED OR REPRODUCED AND WE APPRECIATE YOUR HELP IN PROTECTING OUR COPYRIGHT.

Rising Stars UK Ltd, 7 Hatchers Mews, Bermondsey Street, London SE1 3GS

www.risingstars-uk.com

Published 2010
Reprinted 2010, 2011

Text, design and layout © 2008 Rising Stars UK Ltd.

Editorial: Dodi Beardshaw and Marieke O'Connor
Illustrations: Phill Burrows
Design: Branford Graphics and Clive Sutherland
Cover design: Burville-Riley Partnership

Picture acknowledgements
p12 Tony French/Alamy; p19 Andrew Butterton/Alamy; p22 Gabriel Domenichelli/iStockphoto; pp32 Reza/Webistan/Corbis (top left), Ragne Kabanova/Dreamstime.com (top middle), Raycan/Dreamstime.com (top right), A. Arrizurieta/AFP/Getty Images (bottom), p53 Wolfgang Amri/iStockphoto; pp40 Sean Nel/Dreamstime.com (left), Ian O'Leary/Dorling Kindersley (middle), Dave King/Dorling Kindersley (right).

British Library Cataloguing in Publication Data.
A CIP record for this book is available from the British Library.

ISBN: 978 1 84680 684 1

Printed by Craft Print International Ltd, Singapore

Contents

What are writing skills?

Did you know that teachers are helping you to develop your writing in at least seven different ways? These are called 'assessment focuses' (AFs). They are described here:

★ **AF1:** Write imaginative, interesting and thoughtful texts.

★ **AF2:** Produce texts which are appropriate to task, reader and purpose.

★ **AF3:** Organise and present whole texts effectively, sequencing and structuring information, ideas and events.

★ **AF4:** Construct paragraphs and use cohesion within and between paragraphs.

★ **AF5:** Vary sentences for clarity, purpose and effect.

★ **AF6:** Write with technical accuracy of syntax and punctuation in phrases, clauses and sentences.

★ **AF7:** Select appropriate and effective vocabulary.

The AFs can be grouped together, like this, to make them more manageable to practise:

Sentences: Construct complex sentences, including use of connectives, adjectives, adverbs and punctuation. AF5/6/7

Paragraphs: Organise your writing. AF3/4

Whole text: Develop ideas, think about the needs of a reader, use interesting vocabulary and an appropriate style. AF1/2

These writing skills fit together, like bricks in a wall, to make your written work strong and successful.

Connectives	adjectives and adverbs	punctuation
paragraph organisation	topic sentences	links between paragraphs
relevant and developed ideas	clear signals to the reader	vocabulary to suit the topic

Why use this book?

This book will help you to move your writing skills up from one National Curriculum level to another. For example, if you are currently working at level 3, advice and exercises will help you to progress to level 4, or 5.

- **Knowing what you need to do** to achieve your target level is also essential so we explain and give examples of what you need to be able to do.
- We know that students **learn by doing** so practice is an important part of the book.

The book includes the following features to make it easy to use and to highlight what you really need to be able to do.

(1) **Target level statement** – this tells you what you need to do to achieve the next level in your reading skill.

(2) **Assessment focus** – this identifies the main writing skill that is being practised. See page 4 for more information.

(3) **Tips** – these give you helpful hints, similar to how your teacher does in class.

(4) **Writing practice tasks** – varied exercises to help you practise language skills.

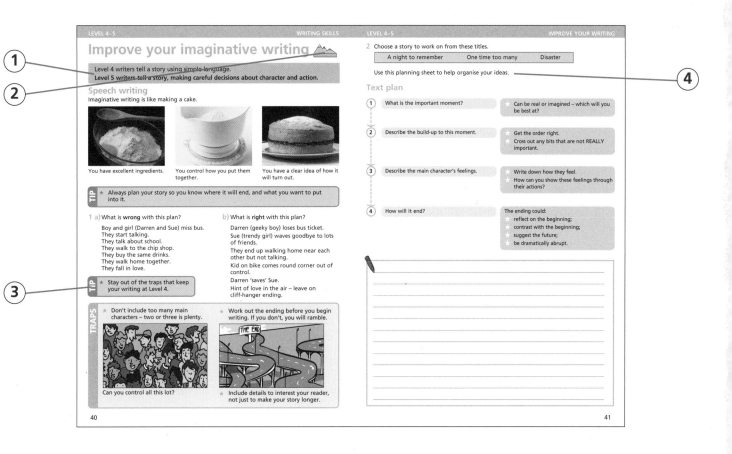

How to use this book

★ You can use the sections in this book to work on the writing skills you need to practise. Or, work through the whole book for overall improvement. The following sections will help you to practise one skill at a time. This approach helps you to focus closely on each element of writing so that you can improve your overall standard of writing when you combine all the skills together.

TIP
★ Ask your teacher for advice on which writing skills to practise first.
Your teacher will be pleased you are making a special effort to improve!

★ Each section targets a different writing skill and practises the skill in a variety of ways across levels 3, 4 and 5 so that you can learn the 'extra' things you need to understand and do for each level.

★ Practise in short bursts of activity and **do** read the advice first so that you focus on the writing skill, not just answering the questions.

TIP
★ 'Warm up' by doing an exercise at your current writing level before trying the exercises to move you up to the next level.

★ Use the **self-assessment sheets** on pages 44 and 45 to identify the level at which you are writing.

Sentence structure and punctuation

★ **Connectives** (pages 8–11) writers at:
Level 4 use a limited range of connectives.
Level 5 use a wider variety of connectives and sometimes use them to begin a sentence.

★ **Adjectives** (pages 12–15) writers at:
Level 4 add detail by using some interesting adjectives.
Level 5 add detail with interesting adjectives and longer phrases and clauses.

★ **Adverbs** (pages 16–19) writers at:
Level 4 use simple adverbs.
Level 5 use a wider range of adverbs and some adverbial phrases.

★ **Punctuation** (pages 20–23) writers at:
Level 4 can use certain kinds of punctuation accurately.
Level 5 use a wider range of punctuation accurately.

Text structure and organisation

★ **Paragraph and text organisation devices** (pages 24–27) writers at:
Level 4 can organise their ideas around a main – or topic – sentence in a paragraph.
Level 5 give clear openings and closings to their writing and make links between sections.

Using an appropriate style for the task and the reader

Practice and helpful techniques to improve your writing in a range of different styles:

★ **Informative writing** (pages 36–37) writers at:
Level 4 use clear and simple language.
Level 5 choose language to inform and interest the reader.

★ **Persuasive writing** (pages 38–39) writers at:
Level 4 give their ideas about a topic.
Level 5 use some techniques to influence a reader.

★ **Imaginative writing** (pages 40–41) writers at:
Level 4 tell a story, using simple language.
Level 5 tell a story, making careful decisions about character and action.

★ **Writing to review** (pages 42–43) writers at:
Level 4 explain opinions simply.
Level 5 explain opinions clearly and politely.

Developing your writing skills

Understanding **what** to practise is very important to your progress. Use this table to plan your improvement and identify what you want to do first.

| | skill | I can | I want to do this | | | |
		Level 3	Level 4	pages	Level 5	pages
sentences	Connectives	use connectives including *and, but* and *because*	use a range of connectives, including *when* and *if*	8–9	use a wider variety of connectives and sometimes use them to begin sentences	10–11
	Adjectives and adverbs	use simple adjectives and adverbs	add detail by using some interesting adjectives and adverbs	12–13 16–17	use longer phrases and clauses to add detail and interest	14–15 18–19
	Punctuation	often use full stops and capital letters accurately	use full stops, capital letters and some commas accurately	20–21	use a wider range of punctuation accurately	22–23
paragraphs	Paragraph and text organisation	use paragraphs, but they need more organisation	organise my ideas around a main – or topic – sentence in a paragraph	24–25	give clear openings and closings to my writing and make links between sections	26–27
whole text	Informative writing	use simple ideas	use relevant ideas and develop some of these ideas use clear, simple language	28–29	choose language to inform and interest the reader	36–37
	Persuasive writing	write about the subject given but do not think about the reader	be aware of the needs of the reader give my own ideas about a topic	30–31	use some techniques to influence a reader	38–39
	Imaginative writing	use simple words	use a wider range of words and try to use some for effect on the reader tell a story using simple language	32–33	tell a story, making careful decisions about character and action	40–41
	Writing to review	write as I would speak to someone	change my style to suit the task explain opinions simply	34–35	explain opinions clearly and politely	42–43

Shade each section when you have completed the exercises successfully.

 TIP ★ Ask your teacher for help in choosing what to do first. Your teacher wants you to improve too.

Using connectives

> Level 3 writers generally use *and*, *but* and *because* to link ideas in sentences.
> **Level 4 writers use a limited range of connectives including *when* and *if*.**

1 Practise using | **and   but   because** | to make a link between the parts of these sentences. It's not as easy as you think!

Turn up the heating …	___**and**___ let's stay indoors.
	a) _because_ it's snowing outside.
	b) __but__ not for too long.
This is a difficult time for Ronesco the footballer …	c) _____ it shows.
	d) _____ he's not scoring any goals.
	e) _but_ he's still scoring goals.
The T-shirt is worn out …	f) _____ I still like it.
	g) _because_ I've had it so long.
	h) _but_ I now wish I'd bought two of them.

2 Now join the beginnings to the end using | **and   but   because** |.

My car is not going very fast _**because**_	it needs repairing.
a) The engine sounds all right _but and_	
b) This car has a flat battery ____ _but_	
c) Simon has bought a new game _____	he wanted one.
d) John saw the new game _and_	
e) Carl didn't ask for the new game _but_	
f) The letters didn't arrive yesterday _but_	they came today.
g) Granny and Grandad won't visit us next week _because_	
h) The builders came to repair the wall yesterday _and_	

TIP

★ The connective **and** is often used far too much in Level 3 writing. Try to use other connectives.

8

TIP
★ Use connectives **when**, **if** and **so**. They are easy to use and help to make your writing more interesting.

3 This is a review about a computer game. It is well-written apart from using **and** far too much. Replace the use of **and** with the connectives given in the boxes that follow.

New Game for Skate Fans

Grind is a computer game about skateboarding and it is the best game I have played on the computer. I enjoyed Grind very much, ~~and~~ a) ___so___ I thought I should pass on my comments.

First you click on start ~~and~~ b) ___then___ you choose who is going to take part in the competition. You can choose famous skateboarders ~~and~~ c) ___or___ you can make up your own names if you want. It's up to you. The computer sets up a course for you ~~and~~ d) ___but___ you can create your own course. I think it is better to do it yourself ~~and~~ e) ___because___ that might be because I have played it a lot. I try to put in lots of difficult jumps ~~and~~ f) ___so___ it's more exciting.

or	or	but	because	then	so

The game can seem easy ~~and~~ g) ___so___ be careful because you lose points for every mistake. You lose points if you lose the board ~~and~~ h) ___but___ go round the course the wrong way. The lowest number of penalty points wins and my best score is 23.

I am into skateboarding ~~and~~ i) ___so___ that could be why I liked Grind. I would definitely recommend it to people ~~and~~ j) ___but___ only if they like skateboarding. If you do, then it's a great game!

so	or	but	but

TIP
★ Don't use the same connective in two sentences next to each other.

4 Write about your favourite way to spend a day using as many different connectives as you can.

Level 4 writers use a limited range of connectives.

Level 5 writers use a wider variety of connectives and sometimes use them to begin a sentence.

When you are writing, using a variety of words will keep your reader interested.
We all get bored of the same thing time after time ...

Oh no. Let me guess ...

Fish and chips, your favourite!

Chips and sausage today, son!

Chips for tea tonight.

5 Look at these charts of beginnings and endings of sentences.
   Use a different connective each time to link both parts of the sentence.

Beginning			Ending	Connective
The school team is doing well this season, ...	a)	_____**although**_____	... we expected they'd do badly.	but
	b)	_____	... they have a new goalkeeper.	because
	c)	_____	... they have a tough game on Friday.	although
Mum, I'm not wearing these any more, ...	d)	_____	... they are still comfortable.	because
	e)	_____	... they are not trendy.	if
	f)	_____	... that's ok with you?	although

6 How many connectives COULD join the sentences below and make sense? Write as many as you can.

   ★ Fred needed a girlfriend.

   ★ Nobody seemed to fancy him.

TIP

★ Good writing uses a wide range of connectives – including *and* and *but*. Simple sentences with no connectives work too. Variety is the key to success.

7 This writing is about a trip to a castle. The sentences are all very short.
Improve the level of the writing by joining SOME of the sentences together. One is done for you.

DO USE	DO NOT USE
where	and
because	but
as	
although	so
if	
after	
even though	

a)

My Nan took me to Tollwood Castle last Saturday. Mum was visiting her sister in hospital.

> Add 1 connective
> **because**

b)

Tollwood Castle has dungeons. You can still see the chains used for prisoners. It was very dark and eerie down there. There weren't any windows.

> Add 2 connectives

c)

We looked around a hall full of very old weapons. We had a coffee and cake. In the shop I bought a book on Tudor armour. Nan said it was expensive.

> Add 3 connectives

d)

After lunch we walked round the gardens. It got much too hot for poor old Nan. She is 62! We went back indoors. She said she might be about to faint. At about half four we went home. Nan was going to karate classes at 7!

> Add 3 connectives

8 a) Write school reports for Amelia and Justin and include as many different connectives as you can. Add your own ideas too.

homework is late   great at English   polite   shy   top student

poor effort   works hard

worst in Maths test   always smart

talks to others   full of ideas   excellent at Science   should put hand up more often

when	where
because	although
while	though
before	even if
after	so that
until	if
so	

b) Use a highlighter to identify all your connectives. How many different ones did you use?

Adding detail by using adjectives

Level 3 writers add detail by using some simple adjectives.

Level 4 writers add detail by using some interesting adjectives.

When you are describing things, you need adjectives to make them clearer and tell the reader more about them.

1 Write down as many words as you can to describe the things in the picture, e.g. colourful clothes.

2 Adverts use lots of **positive adjectives**. If you are selling something, you need to say how **good** your item is so that people will bid for it.

Unworn, stylish pair of knee-high boots.

Choose an adjective from the box below to improve these descriptions.

real	dark	brand-new	clever	useful	coloured	top-quality	cold

trainers	a) _____ skateboard trainers. Light
	b) _____ suede. Size 8.
travel guide	c) _____ guide to Egypt.
watch	One d) _____ watch. Rolex-style with
	e) _____ diamonds.

TIP

★ Avoid using **good, bad** or **nice**. Take time to think of a word to **help the reader imagine** what you are describing.

3 Write adverts for three things that you might want to sell.

> **TIP**
>
> ★ Imagine the situation in your head. Think about how things look.

4   This is a letter of complaint about a holiday that went badly wrong. Fill in the gaps in the first paragraph with negative adjectives from the box. Then choose your own for C–F.

Dear Sirs,

I am writing to complain about my trip with you to Portugal.
Firstly, we were picked up at the airport on a a) [   ]
coach driven by a b) [   ] driver.

> teenage   sensible   modern   battered

When we set eyes on the c) [   ] hotel our hearts sank.   The
d) [   ] girl on the reception desk was as good as useless.
It took us hours to be given our room keys. The e) [   ]
rooms were a disgrace and the f) [   ] balcony was a danger
to the public.

I hope that you will be able to understand how all these problems
spoiled our holiday and that you will refund some of our money.

Yours faithfully
    D. Thompson
D. Thompson

5   Look at this detective story. Choose your own adjective for each gap.

Bill Beat opened the a) [   ] office door. He'd been in the police force
a long time and was a b) [   ] detective. With a keen eye he looked
around the c) [   ] room. There was a table, a d) [   ] stool,
and a e) [   ] mirror hanging on the wall. Not many places to hide
a bag of diamonds! He knew they had to be in there, but where? He whistled
thoughtfully. Then it dawned on him! Under the certificate! He lifted it quickly
from its f) [   ] nail. He was right. There was a hole with
g) [   ] newspaper pushed firmly into it. He eased the paper out and
saw a h) [   ] bag. He weighed the bag in his policeman's hand and
whistled again. Then he tipped out the ten sparkling diamonds and whistled for
the third time.

Level 4 writers add detail by using some interesting adjectives.
Level 5 writers add detail with interesting adjectives and longer phrases and clauses.

When you are describing things, you need adjectives to make them **clearer** and **tell the reader more** about them.

TIP
★ Details can be very helpful – and they make you a better writer!

6   These sentences are about starting school.
Choose adjectives to improve them. Copy out the new sentences.
The first one is done for you.

	Beginning	Adjective options	Choose
a)	I remember feeling nervous as I approached the gates that day.	wooden damaged sad first	3
	I remember feeling nervous as I approached the damaged, wooden gates that first day.		
b)	Miss Sweeting was the teacher the pupils met in Class 1.	new gentle last cosy	2
c)	There were horrors like playtime milk and sitting cross-legged on the floor and no nap on the sofa.	warm cosy tiled after-lunch	4
d)	The walk home with Mum was a relief from the terrors of the infant classroom.	quiet shocking safe noisy	3

TIP
★ In your own writing, use the five senses to help you think of an adjective: touch, taste, sight, smell, hearing.

7 Improve this piece of writing by adding descriptive details to each paragraph.

I hated school. In the Infants I cried all the time – hiding under my comforting coat in the dimly lit cloakroom.

By the age of about ten, I also hated PE. The worst times were if I forgot some part of my kit. That a) _____ box full of b) _____ PE kits was every pupil's c) _____ nightmare and to have to take something from it to wear made my skin creep.

And football too. Each week I tried to avoid that in particular. But, more often than not, I had to take up my d) _____ position in goal. But swimming – now that I could do. I wore my e) _____ badges with pride. Diving into the f) _____ water changed school into a different, g) _____ world.

Sometimes you can use a **clause** to describe something or someone – not just one word. For example:

Mr Baker, who was famous for his sarcastic jokes, commented on Jake's late arrival to the lesson. Strangely, Jake, who always had an answer for everything, just slumped down at his desk.

8 Copy the following sentences onto a separate piece of paper. Add a clause to describe the subject at the beginning of each sentence.

a) Tigger, the cat who _____, twitched his tail angrily.

b) Chris, who _____, set up a fantastic goal to win the match.

c) Laura, who _____, chose a designer pair of glasses.

d) The car, which _____, hit the bollard and span out of control.

e) The boy-band singer, who _____, stood up in court.

TIP

★ Try to include at least one or two clauses like this (beginning with **who, where** or **which**) in your work.

9 a) Write a paragraph describing your first day at school. Include as much description as you can.

b) Read over your work and highlight all the descriptions. Change any that you are not happy with.

Using adverbs and adverbial phrases

Level 3 writers sometimes use simple adverbs.
Level 4 writers use simple adverbs to add detail and organise.

A sailor needs help to find the way across the sea.

A reader needs help to find a way through a piece of writing.

TIP
★ Using adverbs will give order and extra detail to your writing.

1 Use the adverbs in the boxes below to organise and add extra detail to this piece about a science experiment. Some can be used more than once.

a) _____ I collected all the equipment I needed for the experiment.

Then I measured b) _____ 20 ml of water into the flask. I wore gloves

and used tongs to c) _____ hold the flask over the heat. The water

d) _____ began to get hot. As soon as the water began to boil, I

started the timer. I let the water boil for e) _____ four minutes.

f) _____ I remembered that I must not put a hot flask on the bench.

So I carried it g) _____ to a mat to go cold. h) _____ I

looked at the amount of water that was left in the flask and wrote down the result.

Adverbs to give extra detail

| safely tightly ~~luckily~~ approximately exactly |

Adverbs to organise ideas

| firstly finally soon |

2 Adverbs tell us when, where or how something is done.

> Tim finished his work **last night**. (when)
>
> Samantha rode the pony **wildly**. (how)

Highlight the adverbs in each sentence and tick the correct box to show whether they are **when** or **how** adverbs (or both).

	Highlight the adverbs	when	how
a)	The soldiers were waiting patiently in the trenches.		
b)	Major Holme suddenly ordered the attack.		
c)	The cup smashed noisily onto the floor.		
d)	Nina muttered angrily to herself.		
e)	First, Laura carefully cut off her sister's ponytail while she lay sleeping.		
f)	Next, she gently drew a moustache in pen on her face.		
g)	Mrs Derek marched furiously up to the headmaster.		
h)	'My John will soon be leaving here,' she loudly announced.		

TIP

★ Adverbs are not difficult to use. The trick is to *remember* to use them!

3 Write out the alphabet. Think of an adverb for each letter.

A awfully

B bravely

C _____

4 Now continue this short story using as many adverbs as you can. Tick them off on your alphabet list.

The Rescue

Carlo lay down wearily on his prison bed. Hopefully, today would mean a rescue …

Level 4 writers use simple adverbs

Level 5 writers use a wider range of adverbs and some adverbial phrases.

Adverbs are used to add detail about:

 how things happen ➤ Joe **carefully** picked up the injured cat.

 when something happens ➤ **Afterwards,** they went home.

 where something happens ➤ They waited **outside the school gates**.

Adverbials of time add details of WHEN or HOW OFTEN something happens.

This sentence contains two adverbials of time:

Now and then, Kylie would do the washing up after dinner but **most frequently** she just watched the TV.

> ★ You probably use the adverbs below a lot when you speak. Make sure you use them in your writing.

5 Find opposite adverbs for those below. Then, write a sentence that includes both.

Adverb	Opposite adverb
a) never	_____
b) afterwards	_____
c) later	_____
d) occasionally	_____
e) rarely	_____

6 He ran **around the corner** and **through the park gates**.

These adverbials tell us where something happens.
Write a sentence including a phrase that uses these adverbs.

Adverb	Opposite adverb
a) in front of	behind
b) underneath	on top of
c) downstairs	upstairs
d) forwards	backwards
e) towards	away from

7 Using the words in the box below, add details of **where** and **when** to this newspaper report about a whale stranded in the River Thames in London. The first box is done for you.

> last weekend   after a while   up the river   before long   towards the sea
> meanwhile   eventually   into a sling   soon   onto a boat   within minutes   today

Stranded whale rescue fails

The sight of a whale in the River Thames startled visitors to London

| a) **last weekend** |

. Unusually, the whale had tried to make its way

| b) |

rather than

back out to sea.

| c) |

it became very distressed. Divers were

| d) |

called in by the police to help steer the creature

back | e) |

. But,

| f) |

, the divers realised their attempts were making no difference. They tried to lift the whale

| g) |

but it did not survive and they began the task of removing the body. | h) |

people who'd been watching walked away, many of them in tears.

8 Improve this piece of writing with five more adverbs or adverbial phrases telling **when** or **where**.

Jack and Toby had | a) **always** | fancied bungee-jumping.

They had travelled to Hummer Hill, a small tourist attraction, with their

mates. They stood at the base camp and | b) | watched

the jumpers. It seemed a huge drop. | c) | . Toby's heart

pounded | d) | and he felt hollow. 'Bet you're having

second thoughts, mate!' laughed Jack. He knew his brother well.

'I'm up for it, but are you?' said Toby | e) | .

19

Punctuation

Level 3 writers often use full stops and capital letters accurately.
Level 4 writers use full stops and capital letters accurately.

Do you put the lid back on the toothpaste? Millions of people drive others mad by *not* doing this. Why?

Because they are forgetful, they don't care or are just too lazy.

Same with **full stops**. You probably know how to use them, but if you don't use them accurately, your punctuation will not progress to Level 4.

..the crash happened so suddenly the car in front of me stopped to avoid a cat I didn't notice in time the sound of crunching metal

1   Look at these messages. Can you make sense of them?
    Copy them out correctly with full stops, question marks and capital letters.

a)

remember to buy dog food dad wants his dinner early tonight

b)

can you get the hedge trimmer sharpened the hairdresser rang to cancel your appointment

c)

the hamster has escaped again we must get the front door lock changed

d)

the car's got a leak please buy more toilet rolls

2   The story below is well-written apart from the punctuation. Mark the sentences with capital letters and full stops or question marks. The number of sentences needed is given below it.

a) Amina decided to go exploring she made her way past the dustbins and up the narrow alleyway to the Brighton Road.	b) It was a warm day and she felt very lazy she sat on the seat at the roadside a couple of cats were sunning themselves on a wall.	c) She heard a clatter and a bang behind her it sounded like someone had dropped a dustbin lid she turned to see a group of girls watching her they did not look altogether friendly.	d) Amina felt uncomfortable what were the girls up to she decided to stand up and make her way home the group gathered to watch her Amina didn't look back but walked into a shop she did not fancy being alone on the street.
2	3	4	6

TIP   ★   Read the sentences to yourself. This will help you to find the breaks.

3 In this part of the same story the writer has gone mad with full stops! Tick the correct full stops and cross out the incorrect ones. Add capital letters where needed.

a) The leader of the gang seemed to be the small girl. in the black T-shirt. she was chewing gum. and carrying a large shiny red handbag.

b) The other small one was obviously her sister. because their faces were so alike. both had dark brown eyes and. dead straight hair.

c) Would they give her any trouble? Amina smiled nervously and moved past. them back towards the alleyway. and home. she hoped they wouldn't follow her.

d) Her heart pounded. she decided to do nothing but she would ask her cousin about them. later on. she had been silly to go out alone. on her first day. she realised this now.

4 Capital letters are also needed for names – countries, people, brand names, etc.

a) Go through this newspaper article and highlight all the *names* that should have capital letters. Can you find eight different names?

Spider girls trapped

1 Police have arrested two members of one of chile's most notorious gangs they are called the 'spider girls'.

2 The all-girl gang of teenagers is famous for climbing up buildings in santiago their aim is to rob luxury apartments while the owners are out of the city.

3 They lurk in gardens spotting open windows and waiting for their chance they throw ropes up to the balcony railings and climb up the next bit is easy they just walk through the open windows.

4 Between january and august 2005, they made off with thousands of pounds worth of jewellery and clothes by dior, chanel and armani why did they do it because they wanted money for new clothes.

b) Using a different colour highlighter, mark the sentence breaks with a stroke (/).

If you need some help, this table tells you how many sentences there are in each paragraph. But don't look unless you have to.

paragraph	1	2	3	4
sentences	2	2	4	3

TIP

★ Make full stops your main focus for one whole week. You will be surprised at the praise you will get!

Level 4 writers can use certain kinds of punctuation accurately.
Level 5 writers use a wider range of punctuation accurately.

Can you accurately use:

★ full stops?   YES / NO

★ commas to separate items in a list?   YES / NO

★ speech marks, with question marks and full stops?   **YES / NO**

TIP
★ Never forget how important correct full stops are. They are **essential** – not decoration!

Full stops

5 Add eight correct full stops and two exclamation marks to this diary entry.

Monday

I can't believe my luck I was walking to school and I saw something lying in the gutter usually I wouldn't even notice because I'm always listening to my MP3 it broke yesterday so I suppose I was more alert lying there was a wallet I picked it up and opened it up there was loads of cash inside and a driving licence I took it to the Police Station later on they called to say they'd found the owner and he'd left £50 reward for me at the station new MP3 tomorrow I think

Speech punctuation

TIP
★ Remember that the closing full stop goes **inside** the speech marks.

Commas for lists

TIP
★ Remember no comma before 'and'.

6 Add commas to the lists in these sentences.

a)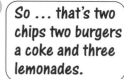
I'm waiting for work from Amish Ben Mark Simon Jenny and Fez.

b)
So ... that's two chips two burgers a coke and three lemonades.

7 Add speech marks and commas to this story. The first are added for you.

Gran is visiting at her grandchildren's house and has lost her false teeth.

'Where do you usually keep them?' asked Jess.

I always put them in the glass beside my bed dear lisped Gran. I can't think where they can be.

Let's start by looking around there then, shall we?

As they went upstairs, Jess heard a clacking noise from her baby brother's bedroom. There he was playing with the teeth!

Clack, clack he chanted.

At Level 5, writers can use commas to separate clauses.

TIP
★ Use commas for sentences that begin with connectives – they are the easiest to spot.

Connective	Comma

If you will eat dirt, you will feel sick!

Connective	Comma

When you are naughty, you will get told off.

Connective	Comma

Although you are a pain sometimes, I'll always love you.

TIP
★ Read the sentences aloud to help you to place the comma. Your voice usually changes for the second clause.

8 Add commas to separate the clauses in these sentences.

> When I get home from school I love to kick off my shoes and sit in front of the TV.
> If my mum is home she usually has different ideas for me.
> Before I can watch TV I have to put away my shoes and tell her about my day.
> While I do that she makes me a drink and a snack.
> Because she knows cheese toasties are my favourite she often makes those.
> Parents, eh!

9 Write a paragraph giving instructions on how to make a cup of tea.
Use these connectives to start some of your sentences and remember to put in the commas.

Before   **After**   **While**   **When**   **If**

Improving the organisation of ideas

Level 3 writers sometimes use paragraphs, but they need more organisation.
Level 4 writers organise their ideas around a main–or topic–sentence in a paragraph.

TIP ★ The first sentence of the paragraph shows the reader what the rest of the paragraph will be about.

1 Draw lines to link the opening sentences to the rest of the paragraph. One has been done as an example.

Opening sentence containing the topic	Ideas which develop the topic

There's too much football on TV.

i) I knew he was ill because he wasn't eating his food. I thought I had better find out what the problem was.

a) I had to take my dog to the vet last week.

ii) The exams have finished and we go on lots of different trips. It's great because we know the summer holidays are about to start.

b) My summer holiday was terrible.

iii) It gets boring after a while. I think different sports should be on. More tennis would be a good idea because lots of people like it.

c) The last week of the summer term is the best.

iv) It rained all week and was really cold. One day our tent was blown down because it was so windy.

2 Write topic sentences for these paragraphs.

a) Mobile phones _____.

Lots of people say that teenagers spend too much time texting their friends, but that's how we communicate these days. Years ago people wrote letters and no one criticised them. We just use mobile phones instead. It shouldn't be a problem.

b) Riding a bike _____.

It gets you from one place to another without harming the environment. It keeps you fit and helps you get to know your home area.

3 Write a short paragraph (about three more sentences) to build up each of these topic sentences.

a) Some people say that your years in school are the best of your life.

b) The issue of testing medicines on animals always gets people arguing.

c) Sport is not for everyone.

4 Read this review. Then highlight the topic sentences and mark paragraph breaks with two strokes (//). There should be four topic sentences and four paragraphs. One of each has been done for you.

STAR SEARCH

Star Search is a new TV programme. It is a talent-spotting show. After the first programme, viewers were invited to visit the show's website and say what they thought about the show. Read this message from the site.

Review

Firstly, there's nothing new in your Star Search programme. There are already loads of shows like that. Three celebrities or stars sit there and vote on who is the best new act. // There is one way it could improve and that is by getting some new stars to be the judges. You need younger and more famous stars to get people to watch it. It needs to be on at a different time. It starts when people are still busy. A lot of people are trying to get home from work or school then. Starting two hours later would be better. I hope you make those changes. If you don't, I think the programme will fail.

> Level 4 writers organise their ideas around a main – or topic – sentence in a paragraph.
> **Level 5 writers give clear openings and closings to their writing and make links betweeen sections.**

A TV company is planning a new series called *Cosmic Cop*. It is aimed at an audience of 12–16-year-olds.

The TV company has shown a pilot programme to a group of teenagers. Here, one of the teenagers, Toni, explains her views.

> You need to change the title. It just sounds stupid. You need to find a title that's a bit more dramatic. It's supposed to be an adventure series for teenagers, not a comedy for eight-year-olds. The main actor is no good. He speaks so softly and you can't really hear him. He really is just too old. You need to make a change there. This pilot episode must have been made with next to no money because it doesn't look real. A few flashing lights and painted cardboard just doesn't convince me I'm watching something real! I think Cosmic Cop is going to be a flop unless you make some serious changes. I hope you will. Toni.

Toni has good ideas, but they are not well-organised.

5   Using paragraphs would make it easier for the reader.

   a) Write **A** in the box below that describes the order of Toni's ideas.

   b) Put a red line (**/**) in the text above where the paragraph divisions should be.

   Those lines will help you see what topics Toni was writing about.

   c) Write **C** in the box that shows a better order for her ideas.

i)	ii)	iii)
The star of the show.	What it looks like.	Make a name change.
What it looks like.	Make a name change.	The star of the show.
Make a name change.	The star of the show.	What it looks like.
☐	☐	☐

TIP   ★   Write a list of your ideas when writing. Then move them around into the best order.

6   Toni doesn't make clear why she is writing or what her viewpoint is. But one of her sentences could be used as an introduction.

   Highlight the sentence that explains why she is writing and gives her viewpoint.

TIP ★ An introduction is important. Use it to make a good first impression on the reader.

7 Improve Toni's opening sentences.

a) For the paragraph about changing the show's title, write a sentence beginning:

First of all, ...

_____

b) For the paragraph about the star, write a sentence opening:

My next comment is not meant to be rude but ...

_____

c) For the paragraph about the set, write a sentence opening:

My final point is about ...

_____

8 Make your conclusion leave an impression on the reader.

a) Highlight Toni's final sentence.

b) Tick the correct button.

i) Does it sound helpful?   YES ◯ NO ◯
ii) Does it sum up the points she has made?   YES ◯ NO ◯
iii) Does it offer hope that the problems can be solved?   YES ◯ NO ◯

c) Write a more developed conclusion that does the three things above.

9 Who makes the best impression? Be smart and organised with your ideas.

27

Developing an idea

Level 3 writers use simple ideas.

Level 4 writers use relevant ideas and develop some of these ideas.

Planning

A good plan helps you to develop ideas before you start.

> ★ Thinking time before you start writing is very important.
>

1 Look at this writing task. Then complete the planning exercises to develop some ideas.

> Your class is preparing a brief information leaflet for new pupils at your school. Your job is to write about school times, food, and what to do if you get lost.

a) Add the ideas given in the box below to develop the main points in this mind map. An example has been given.

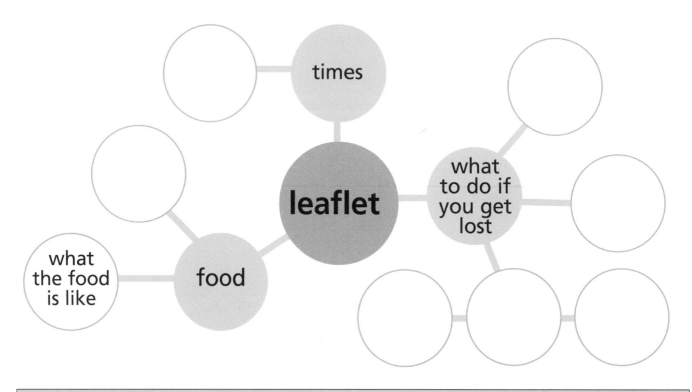

people you can ask for help	what the staff are like	where canteen is
times of the day	information on noticeboards	where the office is

b) Which section has an empty circle?

2 Read this pupil information leaflet to see how ideas are developed into sections.

Welcome to Highlea School	Eating	Lost?
We are a big but very friendly school. You may be a little nervous at first but this information will help you to find your way around.	At break or lunch you can go to the canteen in the school hall. This is through the door to the left of the main entrance.	If you get lost, don't panic. Most people will help you out and some will even show you where to go if they want to miss a bit of their own lesson!
Times	The canteen serves lots of different foods including hot and cold meals. The snacks at breaktime are pretty good and follow the school's healthy eating policy. There are things like baked potatoes, bacon rolls and juices. At lunchtime, they sell a full range of typical school meals. Try the pasta – it's great!	Or, you could go to the school office and they will help.
School starts at 8.45 a.m. Break is at 11.10 a.m. Lunch is at 12.45 p.m. School finishes at 3.45 p.m.		Or, look in your school diary at the map at the back.
		Nearly everybody gets lost once or twice in the first week, so don't worry. Ask!

How many sentences are used to develop:

a) where the canteen is?

b) what kind of food is sold?

c) what to do if you get lost?

TIP
★ Mind maps will help you to see which ideas can be developed.

3 Plan your answers for these writing tasks. Try to develop at least two ideas for each task.

a) On a separate piece of paper, write a description of a place that makes you nervous. Describe:

★ where it is;

★ what it's like;

★ how it makes you feel.

b) On a separate piece of paper, write a letter of complaint to a restaurant. Mention:

★ when you visited;

★ what the food was like;

★ what you want them to do about it.

Writing for a reader

> Level 3 writers write about the subject but do not show that they can think about the reader.
> **Level 4 writers are aware of the needs of the reader.**

TIP
Writing for a reader means thinking about:
★ who the reader is.
★ what the reader needs to know.
★ how to help the reader understand ideas in the writing.

1 When writing the following three emails, how would you treat the different readers?

An email to persuade:

★ your parents to take you to the cinema;

★ your best friends to go to the cinema with you;

★ your teacher to take your class on a trip to the cinema.

Which of these reasons would you use to persuade the different readers? (Some of the reasons could be used for more than one.) Draw lines from the reasons to the readers.

a) I've been really good lately.

b) We haven't been out together for ages.

c) There is a new film of a book we are reading in English.

d) It is a good chance for people to get to know each other.

e) It is quite a cheap evening out.

f) You will love this film.

g) I'll treat you to a night out.

h) It's a film for all ages.

i) We used to love cinema visits when I was little.

Parents

Best friends

Teacher

TIP
★ Writers choose different reasons and different language, because they know the best way to write for different readers.

2 This task is about changes to the school canteen.

The new cook wants to have healthy food in the school canteen. Her idea is to stop selling burgers and start selling tuna sandwiches. But first she wants to know what pupils think, so she has put a box for their comments on the canteen counter.

This is Dave's response for the comments box.

> No one will use the canteen any more, I like my burgers. This idea is stupid. You're trying to force us to eat food we don't like. You can't tell us what to eat. My dad agrees with me and he says you're bossy. Next week I'm going down the road to the burger bar. I hate tuna but I like burger and chips.

a) Highlight sentences about **Dave** in one colour.

b) Highlight sentences about **the food** in another colour.

Dave's comments do not consider the needs of the reader – the school cook! He does not make any positive suggestions; he only writes about himself.

3 Read Adam's response. It is more polite, and also provides the school cook with reasons and ideas that will help her to decide what to do. It considers her needs as a reader.

Label each paragraph with how it helps the reader to understand Adam's opinions.
The first one has been done for you.

A Considers the opposite point of view.

B States his own point of view.

C Explains how burgers could be good.

D Brings ideas to a clear end.

E Adds a new idea to his comment about burgers.

> I don't agree with your plan to stop selling burgers. I think there are lots of reasons for keeping them on the menu. **B**
>
> **1** Firstly, good burgers are not really unhealthy food. It just depends on the meat. If it is low fat meat, it will help us stay healthy. ○
>
> **2** Salad is also healthy and burgers are a good way of getting teenagers to eat salad. The old cook never used to put any salad in the burgers. If you mix the salad with a tasty sauce, we'll be happy to eat lettuce. ○
>
> **3** Your idea for tuna sandwiches might work. Make them taste good and people will choose them. A few people do like fish but most of us want a choice for our dinner. ○
>
> **4** Finally, I hope you will put burgers and tuna on the menu next week. If you do, you will have lots of happy customers! ○

4 Write two letters – one to your headteacher and one to your friend – to persuade them to donate money to your favourite charity.

Using interesting words for effect

Level 3 writers use simple words.
Level 4 writers use a wider range of words and try to use some for effect on the reader.

TIP ★ Do not simply use the first word that comes into your head. Check that it is interesting and adds detail to your writing.

1 Use your *imagination* to think of words about each picture to tell a reader what the *characters* are like. Give at least four ideas for each character.

TIP ★ In a story, the characters belong to you. Give your reader enough information to understand them.

2 Use your *imagination* to add words to describe the *actions* in this picture. An example has been done for you.

glancing back

TIP ★ Using interesting words helps your reader – and gets you good marks!

3 Practise using your vocabulary to add detail to this detective story opening and answer the question below.

Inspector Foreman

Jane Pepper-Davis

Dan Jackson

develop some ideas

elderly, always cleaning
his glasses

rich, attractive, used to
getting her own way

young detective, brainy, a
bit arrogant

Which words do you think best describe these characters? Choose some of the words below to help your reader picture the characters.

old	shuffled	pretty	crafty
glamorous	cross	wealthy	raced
cunning	unhappy	impatient	arrogant
rich	hurried	walked slowly	
bossy			annoyed
in a hurry	elderly	miserable	

TIP

★ One word is not always 'better' than another. The most important thing is to choose the best word for the situation.

Choosing an appropriate form and style

So she said ... and then I said ... and so she said ...

> Level 3 writers write as they would speak to someone.
> **Level 4 writers can change their style depending on the task, e.g. letter, story, newspaper report.**

One main choice of style is between formal and informal writing.

★ Informal – similar to how you speak but not quite the same. You have to give more detail to make up for not being able to use tone of voice or gestures when writing.

★ Formal – think 'posh' or using words as a TV newsreader would!

1 The following exercises are about formal and informal phrases.

   a) Spot the difference between these formal and informal phrases used in letters.
      Mark the phrases with F (Formal) or I (Informal).

Thank you for your letter about ... ⬚ F

Thanks for your letter. ⬚ I

    i)   I'll finish now as I'm running out of space.   ⬚

    ii)   If you have any further questions, please contact me again.   ⬚

    iii)   I look forward to hearing from you.   ⬚

    iv)   I'm writing to ask you a favour.   ⬚

    v)   Write again soon!   ⬚

    vi)   It was lovely to hear from you.   ⬚

    vii)   It was great to get your letter.   ⬚

    viii) Thank you so much for writing.   ⬚

    ix)   I wish to complain about ...   ⬚

    x)   I am writing with reference to your letter ...   ⬚

   b) Are these 'rules' for formal writing true (T) or false (F)?

    i) Do not use abbreviations, e.g. I'm, He's.   ⬚

    ii) Use common words, e.g. want, ask.   ⬚

    iii) Use short, simple sentences.   ⬚

   c) Write out a list of the correct 'rules'.

2 Change these informal sentences into more formal language, using the words in the box to help you. An example has been given.

I've seen a **great** film. **You'll love it**.

I have seen an **excellent** film. **You will be sure to love it**.

a) My dad thinks computer games are rubbish.

b) I'll see you next week.

c) If you want, you can come round tomorrow.

> would like to   father   waste of time   will   look forward to
>
> visit   wish   are welcome to

TIP ★ Most examination writing styles expect you to use a more formal style as it lets you show off your writing skills.

3 Complete a few further exercises on informal and formal styles.

a) Write a brief character summary of your friend using your own, informal style.

b) Now, write a report on your friend by your English teacher.

c) Highlight all the formal language you use in the report by the teacher.

_____

_____

_____

_____

_____

_____

_____

_____

_____

_____

_____

TIP ★ Imagine that you are trying to impress your reader and your writing will generally sound more formal.

Improve your informative writing

Level 4 writers use clear and simple language.
Level 5 writers choose language to inform and interest the reader.

Learning about the passive construction will help you to use formal language when you need to.

Look at this picture of a party gone wrong!

1 Label the picture with what has gone wrong.

What happened	**Passive construction**
Someone broke the window.	The window has been broken.
Someone got out all the DVDs.	The DVDs have been left out of their boxes.

2 Change these sentences to use the passive construction.

a) Someone knocked the books off the shelves.

b) People left plates of half-eaten food all over the place.

c) Someone spilled drink on the carpet.

d) Someone knocked over the table and broke the lamp.

3   Why use the passive construction? Tick True or False.

    a)   It makes your writing sound more formal.   **True** ☐   **False** ☐

    b)   It can add variety to your sentence structures.   **True** ☐   **False** ☐

    c)   It sounds more objective and less personal.   **True** ☐   **False** ☐

TIP
  ★   Passive constructions can make you sound important.

4   Imagine you are a police officer. An elephant from the local zoo has escaped and trampled through the local park.

    a)   Draw lines to link the objects with the damage caused by the elephant. One has been done for you.

> ## had been
>
> | | |
> |---|---|
> | flowers | trampled |
> | swings | destroyed |
> | pond | terrified |
> | ducks | crushed |
> | tables | overturned |
> | benches | emptied |

    b)   Write a report of the damage by the zoo owner.
           Use passive constructions to make it sound formal.

Improve your persuasive writing

> Level 4 writers give their ideas about a topic.
> **Level 5 writers use some techniques to influence a reader.**

Speech writing

1 Look at this speech, which tries to persuade parents NOT to walk children to school.
Complete the tasks to identify how the writer influences the reader.

a) Is this a good introduction? Why?

> Good evening and welcome.
> Now, how many of you walked here this evening?
> If you are not prepared to walk from your homes to this school, why would you expect your children to do so?
>
> Children's health is a hot topic in the news. I know we are a nation of 'couch-potatoes' who love eating crisps and watching TV. But I don't see a problem with this. We are having fun and increasing our knowledge of the world. I really don't think that walking to school will change all our other habits. One little walk to school will not stop the 'damage' the rest of our lifestyle is doing.

> In addition, child safety is also important. Increased traffic on the roads makes them a dangerous place to be. There are many accidents involving children each year. Similarly, the fumes given off by cars and other vehicles can be a danger to children who are walking. At least they are a bit protected when inside a car. Do you really want to put your child in danger?

b) Highlight other phrases that have been used to link paragraphs.

c) Why has the writer used questions?

d) Does this ending link up with any other parts of the speech? Draw lines to show where it links.

> Not only is it dangerous to walk to school, it is also difficult to fit it in. You all lead busy lives and the car is a quick way to get the kids to school and then you go on to work. While you are driving to or from school, you can chat to the children and find out about their day. This means that the car journey actually helps to keep families talking to each other – which is important too.
> To conclude, do you want to put your child in danger and destroy your family by making your child walk to school?

e) How many sentences are there in the main paragraphs?

TIP
★ Level 5 paragraphs will generally need four or five sentences to make sure you explain yourself fully.

Emotive language

Language that appeals to the emotions of your reader works well in persuasive writing. It is known as **emotive language**.

2 Sort these words into two groups: positive and negative words.

> lively   terrible   energetic   dreadful   harmful   dangerous
> wonderful   poisoning   healthy   enjoyable

Repetition

If you have a good phrase, use it twice or even three times to hammer home your message for the reader.

walking works for kids
walking works for you
walking works for all

3 Write a speech to parents at your local junior school persuading them that more children should walk to school.

  a) Use these ideas to get you started and add any of your own.

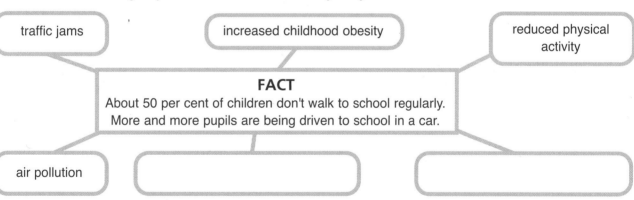

traffic jams

increased childhood obesity

reduced physical activity

FACT
About 50 per cent of children don't walk to school regularly.
More and more pupils are being driven to school in a car.

air pollution

  b) When you have written your speech, tick which of these ingredients you have included.

| an opening that gets a reader's attention | emotive language to get a reaction from your reader | a conclusion that leaves the reader with a powerful impression of your ideas |

| questions to engage your reader | repetition to emphasise a key point | linking sentences to help your reader follow your ideas |

If you have three or more of these ingredients, you will have achieved a Level 5.

Improve your imaginative writing

> Level 4 writers tell a story using simple language.
> **Level 5 writers tell a story, making careful decisions about character and action.**

Speech writing

Imaginative writing is like making a cake.

You have excellent ingredients.

You control how you put them together.

You have a clear idea of how it will turn out.

> **TIP**
> ★ Always plan your story so you know where it will end, and what you want to put into it.

1 a) What is **wrong** with this plan?

> Boy and girl (Darren and Sue) miss bus.
> They start talking.
> They talk about school.
> They walk to the chip shop.
> They buy the same drinks.
> They walk home together.
> They fall in love.

> **TIP**
> ★ Stay out of the traps that keep your writing at Level 4.

b) What is **right** with this plan?

> Darren (geeky boy) loses bus ticket.
> Sue (trendy girl) waves goodbye to lots of friends.
> They end up walking home near each other but not talking.
> Kid on bike comes round corner out of control.
> Darren 'saves' Sue.
> Hint of love in the air – leave on cliff-hanger ending.

> **TRAPS**
> ★ Don't include too many main characters – two or three is plenty.

Can you control all this lot?

> ★ Work out the ending before you begin writing. If you don't, you will ramble.

> ★ Include details to interest your reader, not just to make your story longer.

2 Choose a story to work on from these titles.

| A night to remember | One time too many | Disaster |

Use this planning sheet to help organise your ideas.

Text plan

1 What is the important moment?

★ Can be real or imagined – which will you be best at?

2 Describe the build-up to this moment.

★ Get the order right.
★ Cross out any bits that are not REALLY important.

3 Describe the main character's feelings.

★ Write down how they feel.
★ How can you show these feelings through their actions?

4 How will it end?

The ending could:
★ reflect on the beginning;
★ contrast with the beginning;
★ suggest the future;
★ be dramatically abrupt.

Improve your writing to review

Level 4 writers explain opinions simply.
Level 5 writers explain opinions clearly and politely.

The owners of a large shopping mall are concerned that too many teenagers are meeting there. They have handed out leaflets asking customers to comment.

Improvements to Riverside Shopping Mall

Many users of the Riverside Mall have complained that they have felt threatened by groups of unruly teenagers. To improve this situation we could:

❏ **ban groups of more than three teenagers;**
❏ **ban the wearing of hooded clothing;**
❏ **allow only people over 30 to use the central seating area.**

We would like to hear from all users of the mall.

Your comments for the manager can be posted in the yellow suggestions box next to the main entrance.

1 You and your friends regularly visit the mall at weekends and holidays. You feel these ideas are unfair. You go home to think about how to reply.

a) Identify the points you will need to reply to.

b) Highlight any language you want to use or disagree with.

> TIP
> ★ A quick plan makes sure you include the most important points. Then, when you are writing, you can focus on your language.

2 Write a plan of what you will include in each paragraph of your response.

> **TIP**
> ★ As a general rule, you need at least four sentences for a Level 5 paragraph, so plan to develop your ideas.

3 You must make a good impression on your reader.
Make sure you sound polite.

Highlight the more polite phrase in each of these pairs.

a) I want to … / I would like …

b) Please consider … / You should think about …

c) It is not a good idea to … / It might be better to …

d) I may have to … / I will not …

4 At Level 5, you should use **topic sentences** to show the reader what will be discussed inside a paragraph. For example, for your first paragraph:

I wish to comment on your ideas for changes to the Riverside Mall.

Write your topic sentences for the other paragraphs you will use.

> **TIP**
> ★ Make sure that all topic sentences do not begin with the same words.

5 Write your comments to the Riverside Mall manager.
Include topic sentences and a polite tone.

_____

_____

_____

_____

_____

_____

_____

_____

_____

6 Read through your work and highlight examples of polite language.

Writing self-assessment sheets

★ Look at the descriptions in the Level 4 section of the table.

★ In your work, find examples of the descriptions in the table.

★ Highlight the description in the table, and an example in your work.

★ If you have at least ten of the Level 4 descriptions highlighted, you have achieved Level 4.

★ In a different colour, highlight what you still need to improve.

Level	Sentence structure	Punctuation	Paragraph organisation	Organisation inside paragraphs	Effect on the reader
4	I use different lengths and kinds of sentences. I use *because*, *when* and *if* to connect ideas inside my sentences. I can refer to different points in time, e.g. past, present and future without mistakes.	Most of my sentences have correct full stops or question marks. I use commas for items in a list. I sometimes use commas to separate two parts of a sentence, e.g. *If you go there, you will see ...* When I use speech, my speech marks are mostly correctly placed.	I use paragraphs to group my ideas. My paragraphs are in a logical order, but I haven't made that order clear to my reader. The opening and closing of my writing is clear.	I use a main idea and then add similar ideas to it. I add new ideas to the main idea using *also* or *then*. I use words such as *Next*, *Secondly*, *Finally* to make a link with the next paragraph.	I sometimes add detail to an idea by developing it in the next sentence. I use some words which interest my reader such as *suggest, attractive, patient*. In both tasks, I remember who my audience is.
3	I mainly use simple sentences. I mainly use *and* and *but* to connect ideas inside my sentences. I sometimes refer to the different points in time, e.g. past, present.	I use full stops and capital letters. Sometimes I use question marks and exclamation marks. I often use commas to join two sentences, when I should use full stops to separate them. I use some speech punctuation if it is needed.	I sometimes use paragraphs. My paragraphs are written as I think them. They are not in a particular order. I have tried to use an introduction and a conclusion.	The ideas in my paragraphs are not in a particular order. I sometimes use words such as *then* or *and* to add ideas. It can be difficult to see how an idea in one of my paragraphs links to the next one.	I give one idea and then move on to the next idea. I use basic words such as *think, chase, large*. In the longer writing task, I sometimes forget I am writing to the headteacher. In the shorter writing task, I sometimes forget I am writing a story for a reader.

★ Look at the descriptions in the Level 5 section of the table.

★ In your work, find examples of the descriptions in the table.

★ Highlight the description in the table and an example in your work.

★ If you have at least ten of the Level 5 descriptions highlighted, you have achieved Level 5.

★ In a different colour, highlight what you still need to improve.

Level	Sentence structure	Punctuation	Paragraph organisation	Organisation inside paragraphs	Effect on the reader
5	I use a variety of different sentence types. I use different openings for my sentences, e.g. *I think … The train stopped … If …*, etc. I use connectives such as *although*, *while* and *even if* to link ideas in my sentences.	The ends of my sentences are correctly punctuated. When I use speech punctuation, I place the commas correctly. I use commas to mark clauses for sentences beginning with *Although …*, *Because …*, *If …*, *When …*, etc.	The order of my paragraphs is logical, e.g. most important to least important points/clear time sequence. My conclusion links to my introduction or the main idea of the text, e.g. by summarising in an argument or tying up loose ends in a story.	My paragraphs have a main point and a number of smaller points on the same topic. My paragraph openings give clear signals to the reader, e.g. a topic sentence. I sometimes make links between paragraphs, e.g. *Later …*, *In addition …*, etc.	I develop my ideas across a number of sentences. I use a range of interesting words that make my ideas clear, e.g. *worthwhile*, *recommend*, *suitable*. I recognise my audience by using words which suit the task, e.g. *to be polite*, *to persuade*.
4	I use different lengths and kinds of sentences. I use *because*, *when* and *if* to connect ideas inside my sentences. I can refer to different points in time, e.g. past, present and future without mistakes.	Most of my sentences have correct full stops or question marks. I use commas for items in a list. I sometimes use commas to separate two parts of a sentence, e.g. *If you go there, you will see …* When I use speech, my speech marks are mostly correctly placed.	I use paragraphs to group my ideas. My paragraphs are in a logical order, but I haven't made that order clear to my reader. The opening and closing of my writing is clear.	I use a main idea and then add similar ideas to it. I add new ideas to the main idea using *also* or *then*. I use words such as *Next*, *Secondly*, *Finally* to make a link with the next paragraph.	I sometimes add detail to an idea by developing it in the next sentence. I use some words which interest my reader such as *suggest*, *attractive*, *patient*. In both tasks, I remember who my audience is.

Pages 8–9: Using connectives (L3–4)

1 a) because b) but c) and d) because e) but
   f) but g) because h) and
2 a) but b) and c) because d) and e) but f) but
   g) because h) and
3 a) so b) then c) or d) or e) but f) because g) but
   h) or i) so j) but
4 *Check this with your teacher.*

Pages 10–11: Using connectives (L4–5)

5 a) although b) because c) but d) although
   e) because f) if
6 and/but/because/although
7 a)–d) *Check your answer with your teacher.*
8 a)–b) *Check your answers with your teacher.*

Pages 12–13: Adding detail by using adjectives (L3–4)

1 *Check your answers with your teacher.*
2 a) brand-new, top-quality b) coloured
   c) useful, brand-new d) top-quality, brand-new
   e) real, top-quality, coloured
3 *Check your answers with your teacher.*
4 a) battered b) teenage c) e.g. awful, grim,
   run-down d) e.g. hopeless, young, grubby
   e) e.g. dirty, cramped, dark f) e.g. broken,
   wobbly, unsafe
5 a) smashed, broken, cracked b) top-class,
   excellent c) messy d) broken, smashed
   e) cracked, broken f) rusty g) crumpled h) small

Pages 14–15: Adding detail by using adjectives (L4–5)

6 b)–d) *Many combinations are possible.*
7 *The answers here are examples.*
   a) disgusting/huge/smelly
   b lost/smelly/dirty/old/other people's/stinking
   c) worst
   d) usual/normal/least favourite
   e) little/treasured
   f) cold/sparkling/wonderful
   g) better/pleasant/enjoyable
8 *The answers here are examples.*
   a) who usually never got off the bed
   b) who hated football
   c) who loved spending money
   d) which was driven by Grandpa
   e) who had hit the reporter
9 a)–b) *Check your answers with your teacher.*

Pages 16–17: Using adverbs and adverbial phrases (L3–4)

1 a) firstly b) exactly c) safely, tightly d) soon
   e) approximately f) Luckily g) safely h) Finally
2 a) patiently (how) b) suddenly (when)
   c) noisily (how) d) angrily (how)
   e) First (when), carefully (how)
   f) Next (when), gently (how) g) furiously (how)
   h) loudly (how)
3 *Check with your teacher.*
4 *Check with your teacher.*

Pages: 18–19: Using adverbs and adverbial phrases (L4–5)

5 a) always b) before c) earlier d) frequently
   e) often
   Check your sentences with your teacher.

6 *Check your answers with your teacher.*
7 b) up the river c) within minutes/today
   d) soon e) towards the sea f) before long
   g) onto a boat/into a sling
   h) meanwhile/eventually
8 b)–e) *Check your answer with your teacher.*

Pages 20–21: Punctuation (L3–4)

1 a) Remember to buy dog food. Dad wants his
     dinner early tonight.
   b) Can you get the hedge trimmer sharpened? The
     hairdresser rang to cancel your appointment.
   c) The hamster has escaped again. We must get
     the front door lock changed.
   d) The car's got a leak. Please buy more toilet
     rolls.
2 a) … go exploring. She made …
   b) … very lazy. She sat … the roadside. A couple …
   c) … behind her. It sounded … dustbin lid.
     She turned … watching her. They did not …
   d) … felt uncomfortable. What were the girls up
     to? She decided … way home. The group …
     watch her. Amina didn't … into a shop. She did
     not fancy …
3 a) The leader of the gang seemed to be the small
     girl in the black T-shirt. She was chewing gum
     and carrying a large shiny red handbag.
   b) The other small one was obviously her sister
     because their faces were so alike. Both had
     dark brown eyes and dead straight hair.
   c) Would they give her any trouble? Amina smiled
     nervously and moved past them back towards
     the alleyway and home. She hoped they
     wouldn't follow her.
   d) Her heart pounded. She decided to do nothing
     but she would ask her cousin about them later
     on. She had been silly to go out alone on her
     first day. She realised this now.
4 a) Chile's, Spider Girls, Santiago, January, August,
     Dior, Chanel, Armani
   b) gangs // they; Santiago // their; chance // they;
     climb up // the next; is easy // they just; Armani
     // why did; do it // because they

Pages 22–23: Punctuation (L4–5)

5 I can't believe my luck! I was walking to school
   and I saw something lying in the gutter. Usually I
   wouldn't even notice because I'm always listening
   to my MP3. It broke yesterday so I suppose I was
   more alert. Lying there was a wallet. I picked it up
   and opened it up. There was loads of cash inside
   and a driving licence. I took it to the Police
   Station. Later on they called to say they'd found
   the owner and he'd left £50 reward for me at the
   station. New MP3 tomorrow I think!
6 a) I'm waiting for work from Amish, Ben, Mark,
     Simon, Jenny and Fez.
   b) So … that's two chips, two burgers, a coke and
     three lemonades.
7 'I always put them in the glass beside my bed
   dear,' lisped Gran. 'I can't think where they can
   be.'

'Let's start by looking around there then, shall we?' As they went upstairs, Jess heard a clacking noise from her baby brother's bedroom. There he was playing with the teeth! 'Clack, clack,' he chanted.

8 When I get home from school, I love to kick off my shoes and sit in front of the TV.
If my mum is home, she usually has different ideas for me.
Before I can watch TV, I have to put away my shoes and tell her about my day.
While I do that, she makes me a drink and a snack.
Because she knows cheese toasties are my favourite, she often makes those.
Parents, eh!

9 *Check your answer with your teacher.*

Pages 24–25: Improving the organisation of ideas (L3–4)

1 **a)** i **b)** iv **c)** ii
2 *Sample answers:*
a) Mobile phones are a good way of communicating.
b) Riding a bike is a good choice of transport.
3 **a)–c)** *Check your answer with your teacher.*
4 There is one way it could improve and that is by getting some new stars to be the judges. You need younger and more famous stars to get people to watch it. //
It needs to be on at a different time. It starts when people are still busy. A lot of people are trying to get home from work or school then. Starting two hours later would be better. //
I hope you make those changes. If you don't, I think the programme will fail.

Pages 26–27: Improving the organisation of ideas (L4–5)

5 **a)** A in box iii
b) You need to change the title. It just sounds stupid. You need to find a title that's a bit more dramatic. It's supposed to be an adventure series for teenagers, not a comedy for eight-year-olds. / The main actor is no good. He speaks so softly and you can't really hear him. He really is just too old. You need to make a change there. / This pilot episode must have been made with next to no money because it doesn't look real. A few flashing lights and painted cardboard just doesn't convince me I'm watching something real! I think *Cosmic Cop* is going to be a flop unless you make some serious changes. / I hope you will. Toni.
c) C in box ii
6 I think *Cosmic Cop* is going to be a flop unless you make some serious changes.
7 **a)–c)** *Check your answer with your teacher.*
8 **a)** I hope you will.
b) **i)** No **ii)** No **iii)** No
c) *Sample answer:*
I hope my comments are helpful because I would like the show to succeed. If you change the title, the main actor, and put some more money into making it look real, then I think you will be on the way to

success. Just those few changes and you could make it a winner!
Compare yours, then check with your teacher.
9 *Check your answer with your teacher.*

Developing your whole text skills (L3–4)
Pages 28–29: Developing an idea
1 **a)** **times:** times of the day
food: where canteen is
what to do if you get lost: where the office is, people you can ask for help, what the staff are like, information on noticeboards
b) what to do if you get lost
2 **a)** 2 **b)** 4 or 5 **c)** 4 or 5
3 **a)–b)** *Check your answer with your teacher.*

Pages 30–31: Writing for a reader
1 *The answers here are for guidance only. There is no right or wrong answer.*
Parents: a, b, c, e, f, h, i
Best friends: b, c, e, f, g
Teacher: c
2 **a)–b)** All the sentences are about Dave rather than the food itself.
3 1 C 2 E 3 A 4 D
4 *Check your answer with your teacher.*

Pages 32–33: Using interesting words for effect
1 Any ideas will be correct. The important thing is to have the ideas.
2 Four ideas is good. Six ideas is excellent.
3 Any words could be correct. The important thing is to think about word choices.

Pages 34–35: Choosing an appropriate form and style
1 **a)** **i)** I **ii)** F **iii)** F **iv)** I **v)** I **vi)** I/F **vii)** I **viii)** F **ix)** F **x)** F
b) **i)** True **ii)** False **iii)** False
c) Do not use abbreviations, e.g. I'm, He's.; Avoid common words, e.g. want, ask.; Use longer, complex sentences.
2 *Answers will vary but examples as follows:*
a) My father thinks that computer games are a waste of time.
b) I look forward to seeing you next week.
c) If you would like to, you are welcome to visit tomorrow.
3 *Answers will vary but examples as follows:*
a) (Friend's name) is really great. He's always good for a chat and never drops you in it.
b) (Friend's name) is a model student. He is always punctual and works well with a variety of people.
c) *Check your answer with your teacher.*

Improve your writing (L4–5)
Pages 36–37: Improve your informative writing
1 *Check your answer with your teacher.*
2 **a)** The books have been knocked off the shelves by someone.
b) Plates of half-eaten food had been left all over the place.
c) Drink has been spilled on the carpet.
d) The table has been knocked over and the lamp was broken.
3 **a)** True **b)** True **c)** True

4 a)

flowers	trampled/destroyed/crushed
swings	destroyed/crushed
pond	emptied
ducks	terrified
tables	destroyed/crushed/overturned
benches	overturned

b) *Sample answer*:

By the time I arrived at Eden Park, the elephant had been re-captured and safely returned to the zoo. There was extensive damage to the park. The flower beds had been trampled and two nearby swings were crushed. Tables and benches in the outdoor café had been overturned and badly damaged. The pond next to this area had been emptied of water and I was told that many of the valuable ducks had been terrified and flown away.

Compare yours, then check with your teacher.

Pages 38–39: Improve your persuasive writing

1 *Sample answers:*

a) Asking a question gets people's attention. It makes people sit up and realise it's about them, too.

Compare yours, then check with your teacher.

b) Would you expect your children to do so? Children's health is a hot topic …

… to put your child in danger?

Not only is it dangerous to walk to …

c) To get people to think about the answers.

To get people involved.

To make parents feel guilty if they make their children walk to school.

Compare yours, then check with your teacher.

d) *Check your answer with your teacher.*

e) Paragraph beginning: Children's health …   6

Paragraph beginning: In addition, child …   6

Paragraph beginning: Not only is it …   4

2

Positive	Negative
wonderful	terrible
healthy	dangerous
lively	dreadful
enjoyable	harmful
energetic	poisoning

3 a)–b) *Check your answer with your teacher.*

Pages 40–41: Improve your imaginative writing

1 a) not enough detail to interest the reader; nothing exciting to capture interest; not much point to the story.

b) the characters are more detailed and real; more detail in story to interest the reader; more excitement; some point to the story … Sue realises shouldn't judge by appearances.

2 *Check your answer with your teacher.*

Pages 42–43: Improve your writing to review

1 a) banning groups of more than three teenagers; banning the wearing of hooded clothing; allowing only people over 30 to use central seating area

b) e.g. threatened; unruly teenagers

2 *Check your answer with your teacher.*

3 a) I would like …

b) Please consider …

c) It might be better to …

d) I may have to …

4 *Sample answers:*

Banning groups of more than three teenagers is going to be hard to do and bad for business.

Next, not everyone who wears a hood is a trouble-maker.

Finally, finding out just who is under 30 years old is going to be impossible.

Compare yours, then check with your teacher.

5 *Sample answer:*

Thank you for allowing me to comment on your proposals to 'improve' the Riverside Shopping mall. Like many teenagers, I use the mall regularly. In all the times I have been there I have never seen groups of 'unruly' teenagers.

I admit that groups of teenagers do go around together and have fun but they don't threaten people. You say you are going to ban groups of more than three. So what happens when we come in on our own and meet up with friends in there? Are you going to have security staff everywhere? Anyway, groups of teenagers are some of your best customers. Making it difficult for us to be there is going to be bad for business.

Next, not everyone who wears a hood is a trouble-maker. Hoods are a fashion item for lots of people, young and old. Toddlers wear hoods, so will their parents be told to stop using them? Older people also wear hoods, especially in cold weather. Many people, not just teenagers, might stop visiting the mall if they think they can't wear the clothes they like.

Finally, finding out just who is under 30 years old is going to be impossible. Is everyone going to have to carry an identity card to prove their age? You would have to do that because I don't know how you could tell apart someone who was 28 and 31. This idea is just not practical.

I realise you want to improve, but your ideas are not the way to do it. Let's have a suggestion box for how to make the mall a more welcoming place for everyone.

Compare yours, then check with your teacher.

6 *See highlights above and compare with your own.*